GET CRAFTY

IN THE KITCHEN

Vivienne Bolton

DP

DEMPSEY
PARR

Editor
Barbara Segall

Art Direction
Full Steam Ahead

Design Team
Design Study

Photography
Patrick Spillane

Photographic Co-ordinator
Liz Spillane

Styling
Bianca Boulton

Project Management
Kate Miles

The publishers would like to thank Inscribe Ltd., Bordon, Hants. for
providing the art materials used in these projects and
Sophie Boulton for her assistance.

First published in 1998 by
Dempsey Parr
Queen Street House, 4–5 Queen Street, Bath
BA1 1HE

24681097531

Produced by Miles Kelly Publishing Ltd
Unit 11, Bardfield Centre, Great Bardfield, Essex CM7 4SL

British Library Cataloguing-in-Publication Data
A catalogue record for this book is available from the British Library.

ISBN 1-84084-398-5

Printed in Italy

IN THE KITCHEN

Contents

Plant Pots

Don't throw away those empty yogurt cartons and margarine tubs; recycle them into these stylish plant pots. Create a set of matching planters for the kitchen windowsill using bright, eyecatching colors and white dots and plant useful herbs in them. A design of white hearts or flowers would look good in the bedroom with a leafy, green plant in it, or you could follow the step-by-step instructions and paint a green planter decorated with leaves and flowers.

1 Paint on the base coat. Be sure to cover the pot completely. When it is dry check that the paint is even. You may need two coats to cover the pot well.

2 Paint a thin border at the base of the pot, then paint the rim. When this is dry, paint on the leaves in the same color.

3 Practice painting the flowers on a sheet of rough paper before you paint them on your pot.

4 When flowers are completely dry, paint on the white and yellow centres.

5 These yellow yogurt cartons don't need much decorating. Paint them in bright colors to grow cress in or use them for small plants.

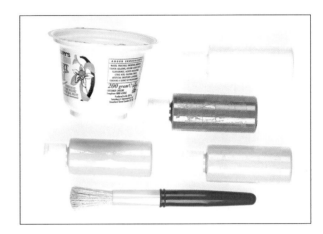

You will need:

A selection of recycled pots and tubs

Acrylic paint in a variety of colors

Paintbrushes

Paper towel or a cloth in case of spills

Acrylic paint will not stick to the tubs and pots unless they are spotlessly clean. Wash all your recycled pots in warm soapy water and rinse them well before drying them with a clean cloth.

Cover your work surface with newspaper before you begin painting.

VEGETABLES, MEAT, AND FISH
Burgers

Follow our easy recipes for burgers that are quick to prepare and delicious to eat. Make them from ground meat, cooked beans, tofu, or fish. There is a recipe to suit every taste. For a professional look, serve your burgers with a garnish such as a slice of lemon, cress, or sliced tomato and lettuce.

You will need:

Ingredients

Bowl

Potato masher

Wooden spoon

Frying pan

Plates and cutlery to serve

Bean Burgers:

1 can of black-eyed beans

1 small chopped onion, fried

1 teaspoon mixed herbs

1 egg

1 cup of brown breadcrumbs

Flour to roll the finished burgers in

A little oil for frying

Tofu Burgers:

8 oz. block of tofu, chopped

1 small chopped onion, fried

2 teaspoons fresh or dried parsley

1 cup brown breadcrumbs

2 teaspoons soy sauce

Sesame seeds to roll finished burgers in

A little oil for frying

Fish burgers:

8 oz. can of red salmon

1 cup brown breadcrumbs

1 small chopped onion, fried

1 teaspoon mixed herbs

1 egg

Flour to roll the finished burgers in

A little oil for frying

Beef burgers:

8 oz. ground beef

1 teaspoon mixed herbs

salt and pepper to taste

1 egg

half a cup of wholemeal breadcrumbs

Flour to roll the finished burgers in

A little oil for frying

1 Empty the beans or other main ingredient into the bowl and mash them well.

2 Add the rest of the ingredients and mix well with a wooden spoon. Use your hands to shape the mixture into burger shapes and roll in flour.

3 Fry in a little hot oil, serve on a burger bun. A tasty meal, easily prepared.

Always have an adult in the kitchen when you are cooking on top of the stove.

Wash your hands before preparing food.

FOIL
Frames

Frame a special photograph in one of these pretty frames. They are made out of cardboard from a grocery box and covered with aluminum foil. Choose a simple shape and expect a few discards while you master the method. Simple patterns are best to decorate the frames: flowers, hearts, or stars, for example. Have a look around the kitchen and you may find colored foil you could recycle. The gold foil frame is made with recycled margarine tub foil! Try sprucing up an old picture frame by covering it with foil.

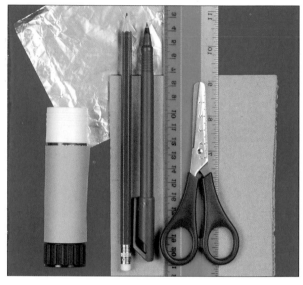

You will need:

Thick cardboard (from a grocery box)

Ruler

Strong scissors

Foil

Glue

Pencil and ballpoint pen

Remember foil is made from metal and can be sharp—take care.

1 Use a photograph to measure how large the frame should be. Cut out the foil shape an inch larger than the cardboard frame.

4 Attach the frame to the backing with glue on three sides, leaving an opening to slip in the photograph.

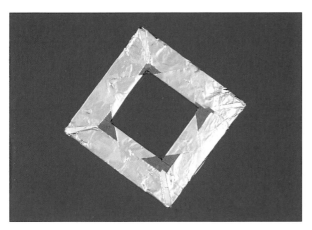

2 Spread the cardboard frame with glue and making sure there is no glue on your fingers, gently press the foil over the frame. Tuck the edges in well, smoothing the foil carefully.

5 Use the ballpoint pen to mark the design onto the frame.

3 Cover the backing of the frame with foil.

PEPPERMINT AND CHOCOLATE
Candy

You will need:

12 tablespoons of icing sugar

1 egg-white

Peppermint flavoring

Green food coloring

Wooden spoon

Bowl

Knife and board

Plain chocolate

Small bowl

Foil

Tray

Glacé cherries

Homemade candy is fun to make and delicious to eat! Try your hand at chocolate-dipped peppermints or cherries. The fruit is made from marzipan and painted with food coloring. You may find that making them takes a little practice, but once you have mastered the art you could make a bowl of miniature marzipan fruit. Have a look at some real fruit for inspiration. Fresh fruit can also be dipped into chocolate—try it with some orange segments.

1 Place the icing sugar, egg-white, 4 drops peppermint flavoring, 12 drops green coloring into a bowl and mix well. You may need to add a little more icing sugar. Knead the mixture for a few minutes until it forms a smooth ball.

4 To make chocolate-dipped cherries, first wash the syrup off the glacé cherries. Pat them dry with kitchen towel and use a cocktail stick to dip them into the melted chocolate. Decorate the dipped cherries with a small piece of cherry.

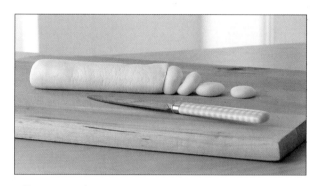

2 Form the mixture into a sausage shape and slice into disks. Use your hands to shape the disks into round candy shapes and place on a board to dry.

Always wash your hands before you handle food.

Remember to tidy up as you go along.

3 Ask an adult to melt the chocolate in a small bowl. Dip the dry peppermints into the melted chocolate until they are half covered. Place the chocolate dipped peppermints on a foil-covered tray to set.

Egg Cups

Boiled eggs for breakfast will never be the same again with one of these fun egg cups. They are made from air-hardening clay. Make a Humpty Dumpty egg cup for a young brother or sister, or choose a more stylish crown or simple shape painted to match your breakfast plates. Make a set of egg cups, one for each member of the family, decorated to suit their hobbies or interests.

You will need:

A block of air hardening clay

Clay modeling tool

Tray to stand the egg cup on while it is drying

Acrylic paints

Paint-brush

Varnish

1 Begin by shaping a block of clay to be the wall for Humpty to sit on.

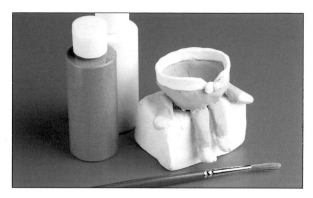

3 When the model is completely dry, you can decorate it. Paint one color at a time allowing each shade to dry.

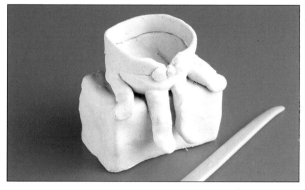

2 Make the legs and arms from sausage shapes and use an egg to gauge the size of the cup. Once you have made your model, leave it to dry for 24 hours.

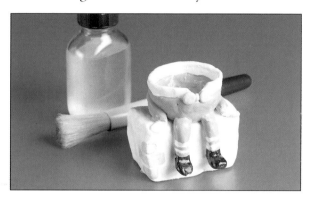

4 Varnish the egg cup when the paint is completely dry.

Before you begin, cover your work surface with newspaper or a plastic cloth—working with clay can be messy. It is a good idea to work on a tray which will enable you to carry your finished item to a safe place to dry.

If you cannot get hold of air hardening clay, make Humpty from salt and flour dough: mix 2 cups of flour and 1 cup of fine salt, add 1 cup of water and mix well. Knead for 5 minutes, then the dough will be ready for use.

SALT AND FLOUR
Dough Baskets

U se salt and flour dough to make a basket for bread rolls or fruit. Once baked in the oven the basket is ready for you to paint and varnish. Flower shapes or dough fruit make very good decoration. Use animal-shaped cookie cutters to make dough pets with the leftover dough. Always bake the pieces thoroughly and allow them to get quite cold before you paint them.

Salt and flour dough is not good to eat, so keep it away from young brothers and sisters.

Always wash out your paint and varnish brushes, to keep them clean and ready to use.

You will need:
Wooden spoon and large bowl

2 cups of flour

1 cup of salt

1 cup of water

A little spare flour

Rolling pin

Knife

Shallow oven-proof dish

Aluminum foil to line your dish

Acrylic paint and brushes

Water-based varnish

4 Bake the basket for 4 hours at 275°F, or until it is completely dry.

1 Use a wooden spoon to mix the flour, salt, and water well. When it forms a ball take it out of the bowl and knead it for 5 minutes. Sprinkle some flour onto the work surface to prevent the dough sticking as you work.

5 When your model is cool take it out of the bowl, paint and varnish.

2 When the dough is smooth roll it out onto a floured surface and cut it into strips about an inch wide.

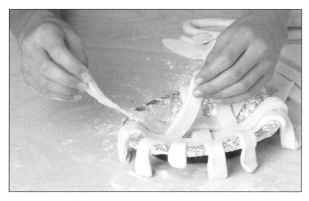

3 Cover a bowl with aluminum foil. Weave the strips into the bowl. Make the cherries from small balls of dough. Use a short piece of thin wire or two small sticks for the cherry stalks.

Toast Racks

Brighten up the breakfast table with one of these easy-to-make toast racks. They are made from recycled grocery boxes and torn up strips of newspaper. Before you begin have a look around the kitchen and choose a color and style that will match.

Some toast racks have space for butter pats and jam while others only have room for toast. When you have made one of the simple shapes you could try something a little different. A nicely made toast rack would make a good gift for a friend or neighbor.

You will need:
Cardboard from a cardboard box

Sturdy scissors

Strong white glue

Water

Torn up pieces of newspaper

Acrylic paint and brushes

1 Use cardboard from a grocery box to cut out an oval-shaped base and four racks. You will need a pair of sturdy scissors.

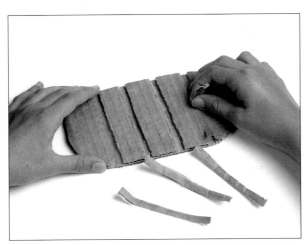

2 Use the blade of the scissors to score the card then tear out slots for the racks. Remember to leave enough space for the slices of toast between the racks.

3 Glue the racks into place and set aside until the glue has dried.

4 Mix an equal quantity of glue with water. Glue small torn pieces of newspaper all over your model.

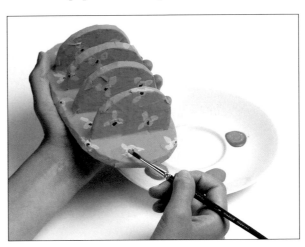

5 When the toast rack is completely dry it is ready to decorate. Use acrylic paint and a design that matches the shape of your toast rack.

Remember to protect your work surface with newspaper or a vinyl cloth.

If you don't have any glue, get an adult to help you make some. Mix two cups of water and one cup of flour in a saucepan and cook it gently, stirring all the time, until it is thick, creamy, and sticky.

Fabric Printing

Decorate a traycloth or table napkins with apple or carrot prints. The prints are made using real fruit and vegetables cut in half. Green peppers make good prints too. Fabric paints come in plenty of colors and are easy to use—follow the directions written on the container. Always try your design out on a piece of scrap paper before you print on the fabric to test out how much fabric paint you need.

Protect your work surface with newspaper before you begin. Keep some kitchen towel handy in case of spills.

If you cannot get hold of fabric paint, try using acrylic paint. You will not be able to wash the cloth but it will make a great wall hanging for the kitchen.

You will need:

Vegetables

Knife

Sponge

Fabric paint

Squares of fabric

Cookie cutters

Kitchen towel

1 Cut a carrot in half. Use a sponge to spread a little fabric paint onto the carrot half. Gently press it down onto the fabric. Only press once and do not move it about when you press. Print a row of carrots on the cloth. Leave the printed cloth in a safe place to dry. Follow the directions that come with the fabric paint to set the dye.

2 Cut a potato in half. Press the cookie cutter firmly into the flesh of the potato. Use a knife to carefully cut away the excess potato. Remove the cookie cutter and you have a stamp ready for printing. Pat the stamp dry with some kitchen towel. Use a sponge to apply the fabric paint to the potato cut and print your pattern.

3 Halved apples printed on this green table mat look jolly. You will need to pat the cut surface dry with a piece of kitchen towel. Use the sponge to apply red fabric paint to the apple surface and press firmly down onto the green table mats.

Glass Painting

Glass painting is a great hobby and a good way of recycling empty jars and bottles or personalizing glasses to give away as gifts or use in the home. Glass paints also work well on plastic containers, so collect a few large plastic containers and decorate them for use in the kitchen, for storing dried pasta or beans. Glass paints come in a wide variety of colors and are easy to use. Experiment with simple designs at first. Always try out your ideas on paper before painting on glass. If you make a mistake on the glass wipe the paint off quickly and start again.

1 Before you begin wash and dry the glass. Use the black outliner to mark up the pattern. Be sure there are no gaps for the glass paint to escape through. When the black outliner is completely dry use a dry brush to dip into the glass paint. Wash the brush well between colors and dry it before dipping it into the next color.

2 Use the gold outliner on its own for this stylish look. Think about what will be in the container when deciding on color and design.

3 Save tiny jars to decorate and fill with jam.

Remember to protect your work surface with newspaper before you begin.

Always make sure the glasses and jars are washed and dried with a clean cloth before you begin to decorate them.

OVEN-BAKE CLAY
Fridge Magnets

Liven up the fridge with a bright blue teapot or a friendly teddy bear fridge magnet. These fridge magnets are made from oven-bake clay, which comes in a wide range of colors.

Fruit and vegetable magnets look good in the kitchen, and a bright red apple, containing a friendly little worm, will bring a smile to everyone's face when at the fridge door.

Follow the manufacturer's directions when baking the clay.

Always have an adult present when using the oven.

1 Before you begin, make sure your hands are spotlessly clean as dirt transfers to the clay very quickly and can't be removed.

Knead the clay in your hand until it is soft enough to use. Shape the teapot following the steps in the picture.

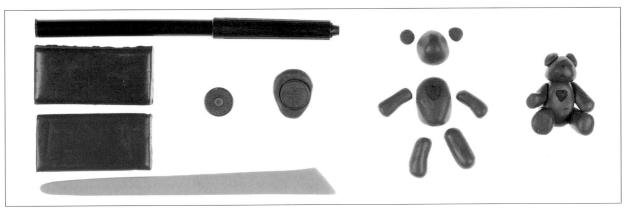

2 The bear is made from dark brown clay. Make his arms and legs from short sausage shapes. Give him a bright red nose, a bow tie, or even a colored hat! If the magnet doesn't stick, glue it on once your model is out of the oven and cooled down.

You will need:

Oven-bake clay in a variety of colors

Knife

Clean surface on which to roll your clay

Small rolling pin or a suitable pen lid

Baking tray covered with foil

Magnets

Glue

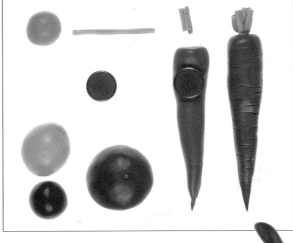

3 This carrot magnet is made from yellow and red clay mixed to give a good orange carroty color. Make the stalk from short rolls of green clay, squashed together.

ROLLS, TURNOVERS, AND PIES
Indoor Picnics

Rainy days are perfect for indoor picnics. Fill the hamper with egg rolls, cheese and potato turnovers, and delicious jam pies. Everyone will enjoy the turnovers which are easy to make and very filling. Use the leftover pastry to make a few jam pies. Simply cut out circles with a cookie cutter, place in a greased shallow muffin pan with a small spoonful of jam in each one. Bake for 12 minutes at 350°F. For the rolls filling, hard-boil an egg and when it is cool, chop it up and mix it with a small spoonful of mayonnaise. Spread it on rolls with some cress for a picnic treat.

You will need:

Bowl

Tablespoon

Rolling pin

Saucer

Knife

Baking tray

Fork

Pastry brush

Recipe for cheese & onion pasties

Pastry:

1 1/4 cups flour

1 stick margarine or butter

A little water

A little extra flour

Turnover filling:

1 cup of cooked diced potato

1 medium onion, chopped

3 oz. cheddar cheese, grated

Salt and pepper

1 egg, beaten

1 Make the pastry first. Place the flour and margarine (or butter) in a bowl, use your fingers to mix it until it looks like breadcrumbs. Add a tablespoon of water and mix well. You may need another tablespoon or two of water but add it a little at a time until the mixture is damp enough to make a ball.

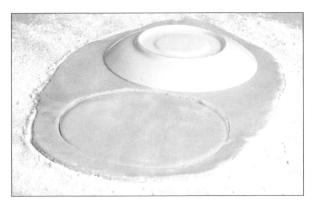

2 Sprinkle a little flour onto the work surface and roll the pastry out to a thickness of a quarter of an inch. Use a saucer to mark out the circles and cut them out with a knife.

3 Place the individual filling ingredients in a bowl. Mix them together well and add a sprinkling of salt and pepper.

4 Place the pastry circles on a greased baking tray. Place a large spoonful of filling in the middle of each pastry circle. Beat an egg in a bowl and brush a little on the edges of the pastry. Fold over the pastry to cover the filling. Use the fork to press down on the edges to seal the pastry parcel.

5 Use the pastry brush to paint egg over each finished turnover. Bake the turnovers for 25 minutes at 350°F.

Always check with an adult before you use the kitchen.

Ask an adult to help when using the oven.

PLAIN AND CHOCOLATE
Cookies

For a special treat, homemade cookies decorated with icing, silver balls cherries, and sprinkles, will brighten up your tea time. Try both recipes (plain and chocolate), cut out in a variety of shapes with a mixture of patterns and designs, to create a colorful plateful of delicious biscuits. A few homemade cookies in a decorative box or bag can make an ideal gift for parents or neighbors.

1 Use a wooden spoon to mix the flour, margarine (or butter), vanilla extract, sugar, and baking powder until it looks like breadcrumbs. Add the egg and mix with a wooden spoon until it forms a dough.

2 Sprinkle a little flour onto the work surface and roll out the dough with a rolling pin. Do not press too hard. Dip the cutters in flour before cutting out a selection of shapes.

3 Place the cookies on a greased baking tray. Bake for 15 minutes at 350°F. Allow to cool and decorate with icing, silver balls, cherries, and sprinkles.

Ingredients

1 1/4 cups plain flour

1 stick margarine or butter

1/3 cup castor sugar

1 teaspoon baking powder

1 egg

For plain cookies add:

1 teaspoon vanilla extract

For chocolate cookies add:

3 tablespoons cocoa powder

You will need:

Wooden spoon

Bowl

Cookie cutters

Cookie decorations

Ask an adult to help when using the oven.

MILK, YOGURT, AND FRUIT
Dairy Drinks

Mix up milkshakes and smoothies in moments using one of these quick and easy recipes. Turn the kitchen into a soda fountain and make drinks for the whole family. The smoothies are made from yogurt and fresh fruit, cooled down with creamy ice cream and the milkshakes are made from fresh milk, ice cream, and fruit. When you have tried these recipes maybe you would like to experiment with different flavors, fresh peaches and raspberry yogurt, or maybe a banana and fudge ice cream milkshake! Remember to decorate your drinks with slices of fruit, whipped cream and paper parasols. Serve with long spoons.

You will need

Blender

Fresh fruit

Selection of ice creams

Milk

Yogurt

Whipped cream

Straws

Decorations

Ask an adult to help when using the blender.

Strawberry milkshake

In the blender place 6 large strawberries, half a small banana, a scoop of strawberry ice cream, and half a glass of milk. Blend well. Serve with whipped cream and a coating of sprinkles on top.

Chocolate milkshake

In the blender place 1 small, roughly chopped banana, a large scoop of chocolate ice cream, and half a glass of milk. Blend well. Serve with whipped cream, two or three banana slices and chocolate sprinkles on top.

Banana smoothie

In the blender place 1 roughly chopped banana, a scoop of vanilla ice cream, and half a glass of natural yogurt. Blend well and serve in a long glass.

Strawberry smoothie

In the blender place 6 large strawberries, a large scoop of strawberry ice cream, and half a glass of strawberry yogurt. Blend well and serve in a tall glass with a blob of strawberry yoghurt and a strawberry on top.

ICE CREAM
Sundaes

Have an ice cream sundae party for your friends. You will need a selection of ice creams, fresh fruit, custard, cream, and decorative sprinkles. Try the home-made strawberry ice cream recipe, since it is quick and easy to make. Fruit yogurts can also be frozen and make tasty ice cream.

Always have an adult present when using sparklers or other fireworks.

Banana and chocolate ice cream sundae

Put one layer at a time into the glass. Start with some sliced banana, then add a spoonful of soft marshmallow. Sprinkle on some chocolate flakes, then a small scoop of vanilla ice cream and decorate with whipped cream.

Strawberry parfait

Begin with a layer of crushed graham crackers. Mix 2 teaspoons of strawberry jam with 2 teaspoons of warm water and pour over the crackers. Follow with soft marshmallow then some chopped strawberries and jelly. Finally decorate with whipped cream and a whole strawberry.

Sparkling ice cream sundae

Place a small tin of evaporated milk in the fridge for 2 hours. Pour the milk into a bowl and use a whisk to whip it until it is light and fluffy. Mix in the strawberries and syrup. Pour the mixture into a freezer-proof dish and freeze until solid. Serve it with a dazzling sparkler.

Index